Reading Essentials® in Social Studies

COUNTRY CONNECTIONS II

RUSSIA

JOANNE MATTERN

Perfection Learning®

Editorial Director: Susan C. Thies
Editor: Mary L. Bush
Design Director: Randy Messer
Cover Design: Michael A. Aspengren
Inside Design: Michelle Glass, Jennifer Beaman

IMAGE CREDITS:

© Peter Turnley/CORBIS: p. 22; © Jay Dickman/CORBIS: p. 27 (top); © Dave G. Houser/CORBIS: p. 28 (bottom); © Rick Barrentine/CORBIS: p. 31; © David Turnley/CORBIS: p. 33; © John D. Norman/CORBIS: p. 35 (bottom); © Bettmann/CORBIS: p. 39 (top); © Reuters/CORBIS: p. 41

ClipArt.com: pp. 5 (top), 9, 17, 18, 19 (top), 20, 37, 38 (bottom); Corel Professional Photos: back cover, front cover, pp. 1, 2–3, 5 (bottom), 6, 10 (top), 12 (top), 27 (bottom), 28 (top), 34, 36, 42; Digital Stock: p. 10 (bottom); Library of Congress: p. 19; MapResources.com: pp. 4, 7, 8, 21; Photos.com: pp. 11, 12, 13, 14, 15, 23, 24, 25, 32, 35 (top), 38 (top), 39 (bottom); Stockfood.com: p. 30

Text © 2005 by **Perfection Learning® Corporation**.
All rights reserved. No part of this book may be used or reproduced,
stored in a retrieval system, or transmitted in any form or by any means,
electronic, mechanical, photocopying, recording, or otherwise, without
prior permission of the publisher.
Printed in the United States of America.
For information, contact
Perfection Learning® Corporation,
1000 North Second Avenue, P.O. Box 500
Logan, Iowa 51546-0500.
perfectionlearning.com
Phone: 1-800-831-4190 • Fax: 1-800-543-2745

1 2 3 4 5 PP 08 07 06 05 04
#36555 ISBN 0-7891-6319-5

TABLE OF CONTENTS

	Just the Facts!	4
CHAPTER 1	Beneath Your Feet—Russia's Land and Climate	7
CHAPTER 2	Living Wonders—The Plants and Animals of Russia	11
CHAPTER 3	Looking Back—Russia's History	16
CHAPTER 4	Digging In to Russia's Resources and Industries	23
CHAPTER 5	The Many Faces of Russia—Discovering Russia's People	26
CHAPTER 6	A Slice of Life—Russian Culture	29
CHAPTER 7	What's Ahead? A Look at Russia's Future	40
	Internet Connections and Related Reading for Russia	43
	Glossary	45
	Index	48

Just the FACTS!

Location

Russia is located on the continents of Europe and Asia below the Arctic Ocean. It is surrounded by several countries and seas. The largest bordering countries are China and Kazakhstan to the south and Ukraine and Finland to the west. The Bering Sea, Sea of Okhotsk, and Sea of Japan line the eastern coast of the country, while the Barents, Laptev, and East Siberian Seas lie to the north.

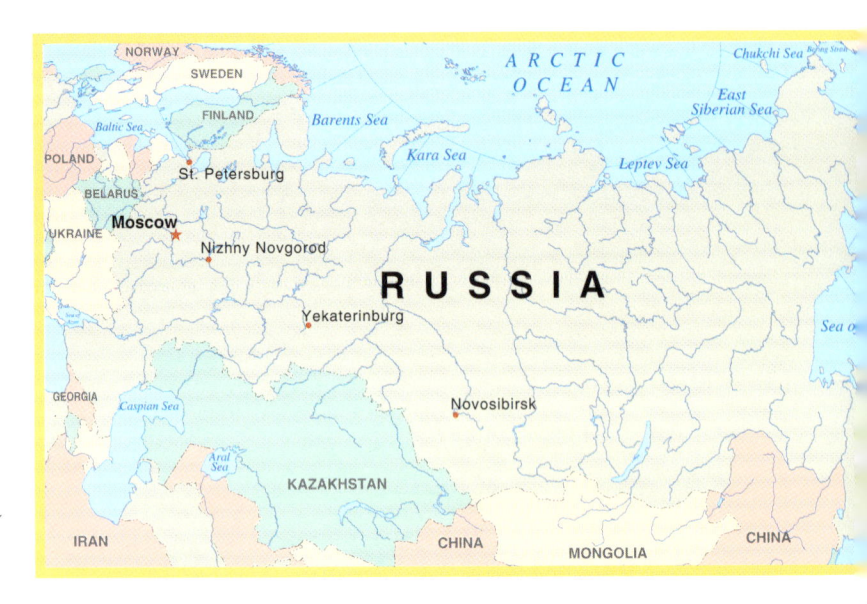

FROM REPUBLICS TO COUNTRIES

Between 1918 and 1991, Russia was known as the Union of Soviet Socialist Republics (USSR). Kazakhstan, Azerbaijan, Georgia, Ukraine, Belarus, Lithuania, Latvia, and Estonia were all part of the USSR during this time. Today, these republics are independent countries that border Russia.

Area 6,592,700 square miles

Geographical Features Western Russia is part of the East European Plain. This area is mostly flat, **fertile** land. The Caucasus Mountains stand at the southern edge of this **plain**. The Ural Mountains to the east of the plain mark the beginning of land that gradually increases in **elevation** from plains to **plateaus** to mountains. The northern portion of this land is frozen **tundra**.

Highest Elevation Mount Elbrus (18,510 feet above sea level)

Lowest Elevation sea level

Climate The climate varies across the huge country. Much of Russia experiences extreme weather conditions—very cold winters and very hot summers. The northern tundra is frozen most of the year. Areas along the southern border are warm and wet, while parts of the southwest are very dry.

Capital City Moscow

Largest Cities Moscow, St. Petersburg, Novosibirsk, Nizhny Novgorod, Yekaterinburg

Population 144,526,278 (2003)

Official Language Russian

Main Religion Russian Orthodox

> **WHAT TIME IS IT?**
> Russia is so large, it covers 11 **time zones**! That means that a person on the far western edge of the country could be having lunch while a person on the far eastern side would be asleep for the night.

Caucasus Mountains

5

Government Russia is a **federation** with a president and a two-chamber legislative (law-making) body.

Industries mining, chemicals, metals, machinery, shipbuilding, communications equipment

Natural Resources coal, oil, natural gas, iron ore, timber, grains

Currency basic unit is the ruble

OFFICIALLY SPEAKING
Russia's official name is the Russian Federation.

MORE FOR YOUR MONEY
One U.S. dollar equals about 29 Russian rubles. You could trade 4 dollars for more than 100 rubles. What a deal!

FLYING CHANGES
Russia has had several different flags during its history. Under **Communist** rule, the flag was red with a hammer, sickle, and star. The hammer and sickle represented the peasants and workers while the star represented unity under the Communist government.

In 1991, the country went back to the flag that had been used before **communism**. This flag has three stripes of white, blue, and red.

A NATION WITHOUT A SONG
Between 1991 and 2000, Russia had no official national anthem. Finally in 2000, new words were written to accompany the music of an old anthem, and the country had a national anthem once again.

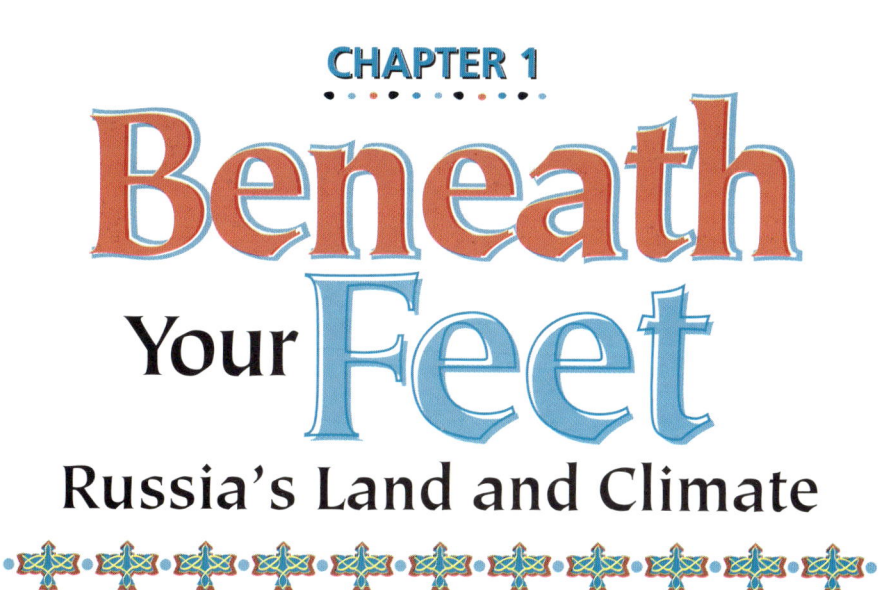

CHAPTER 1
Beneath Your Feet
Russia's Land and Climate

Russia covers more than 6.5 million square miles. The northern and eastern sides of Russia border water, while the western and southern edges border land. The country is part of both Europe and Asia. In fact, it is the only country that stretches across two continents.

SUPERSIZE!
Russia is the largest country in the world in land area. It also has the longest border of any country—22,539 miles!

HELLO, NEIGHBOR
The Bering Sea flows between Russia and Alaska. At the closest point, only 49 miles separate Russia and the United States.

GEOGRAPHICAL FEATURES

Russia has three main geographical regions. The first region covers the part of Russia that's in Europe. This area is mainly flat plains called *steppes*. The steppes are covered with grasses and a few trees.

The Caucasus Mountains rise at the southern edge of the steppes and extend into the region that covers the southern portion of Russia. This region features mountains, plateaus, and deserts.

The third region in Russia is called Siberia. Siberia is located in the north-central and northeastern parts of Russia. The western section of Siberia is flat, swampy lowlands and thick **coniferous** forests called **taigas**. The central part of Siberia is a plateau. The eastern side is mountainous.

ON TOP OF THE WORLD—OR AT LEAST EUROPE

Mount Elbrus, the highest mountain peak in Europe, is located in the Caucasus Mountain Range.

FOREST OF WATER

Taiga is a Russian word meaning "swamp forest." After a long winter in these forests, the snow melts and the ground gets spongy and soggy. Pools of water often dot the forest floor during this spring thaw.

Northern Siberia is frozen almost all year long. This area is known as the tundra. Even in the summer, only the top layer of soil thaws, allowing some small plant growth.

Russia is divided by the Ural Mountains. European Russia is located west of the Urals. Asian Russia is located to their east.

More than 100,000 waterways flow through Russia. The longest river in the country is the Lena. This 2670-mile-long river is located in Siberia. At 2293 miles long, the Volga is the longest river in Europe. The Volga flows south from northwestern Russia until it empties into the Caspian Sea. The Amur, Ob, and Yenisey are other important rivers in Russia.

> **FROZEN IN TIME**
> Parts of the tundra have been frozen for thousands of years. Scientists have found bones and bodies from ancient woolly mammoths frozen under this land.

> **MOTHER RIVER**
> The Volga River is an invaluable source of **hydroelectricity, irrigation,** and shipping waters. Russians call the river "Mother Volga" to honor its significance.

Russia also has the deepest lake in the world. Lake Baikal is located in Siberia. It is 5315 feet deep and holds approximately 20 percent of the world's freshwater.

THE CLIMATE

Much of Russia has a harsh climate. Summers are short and hot. Winters are long and cold. Snow covers the ground for six months out of the year in more than half of the country. Many lakes and rivers near the coast are frozen much of the year.

The tundra in northeastern Siberia is the coldest area in Russia. Much of this land falls within the **Arctic Circle**. Temperatures here often fall below -50° Fahrenheit.

In the winter, cold winds sweep over the open steppes of western Russia. This area also receives large amounts of rain and snow.

The western edge of the country near the Black and Caspian Seas has a warmer climate. Summers are long and hot, and winters are fairly warm. Pockets of land in this area are deserts that receive little rainfall.

The brief summers in Russia can be very hot. Temperatures average in the 70s and 80s but can spike to 90°–100°F. Even the cold northern areas can reach temperatures of up to 95°F in the summer.

Precipitation in Russia ranges from very wet to very dry. Heavy rains fall frequently in the Caucasus Mountains, with up to 100 inches of rain and snow a year. The eastern coast receives up to 40 inches of rain a year. Sometimes tropical storms and **typhoons** travel across the Sea of Japan and strike this area of the country. Other parts of the country, such as the deserts on the western edge, see only about 6 inches of rain a year.

BRRR!

Oymyakon, Siberia, is a very cold place to live. In 1933, this village recorded the coldest temperature on Earth outside of Antarctica—a chilly -90°F.

The eye, or center, of a typhoon is normally the calmest part of the storm.

CHAPTER 2

Living Wonders

The Plants and Animals of Russia

The huge land area in Russia provides many **habitats** for plants and animals. The climate also plays a role in determining where different species are best able to live.

PLANTS

Not many plants can survive in the cold, dry tundra of northern Russia. Trees are limited to a few species of dwarf trees. Most tundra bushes and plants sprout up for just a few days during the short summer season and then die. Mosses and **lichens** grow on rocks and bare ground all year long.

The taiga is covered with fir, pine, and other coniferous trees. Most of these trees have needle-shaped leaves that stay on the tree year-round. The needles have a waxy coating that protects them from the cold. The thin needle shape helps keep the trees from losing water during the long winters.

Moss

Lichen

South of the taiga, there are forests of **deciduous** trees, such as birches, maples, and oaks. In the spring, ferns and wildflowers bloom among the trees. In summer, many grasses, mushrooms, mosses, flowers, and shrubs fill these forests.

The steppes are covered with grasses, small trees, and wildflowers. The soil in the steppes is called "black earth" because of its dark color. This soil is very fertile and can support many crops.

ANIMALS

Animal life in Russia can also be grouped according to habitats. Animals must be tough to live in the frozen tundra. Walruses and seals swim in the cold waters of the northern seas. Polar bears, arctic foxes, reindeer, caribou, musk oxen, and lemmings travel across the frozen ground.

Seal

Snowy owl

The ptarmigan and the snowy owl are two birds that live in Russia's frozen environment. Both birds have white feathers that help them blend in with the snow in their northern home. Ptarmigans' feathers turn brown and black during the brief summer thaw to **camouflage** the birds against the stark land.

The world's largest cat prowls through Russia's Siberian wilderness. Siberian tigers can grow to lengths of more than 10 feet and weigh more than 650 pounds. These fierce predators eat large animals such as deer, wild pigs, and antelopes.

White Siberian tiger

Polar bear

Siberia is also home to musk deer. These deer don't have horns or antlers like most other species of deer. Instead, they have long front teeth that curve downward below their mouths like elephant tusks. These animals do well in cold environments since they eat the grasses, leaves, mosses, and lichens that grow there.

Wolves are some of the fiercest predators in Russia. These animals live in packs that travel across the tundra and taiga looking for food. Wolf packs often attack herds of reindeer or caribou. They swallow meat in large chunks, barely chewing it.

Elk, wolves, brown bears, lynxes, sables, muskrats, squirrels, and foxes live in the taiga forests. Owls, hawks, and nightingales fly through the forest skies.

Bears, deer, boars, foxes, and minks roam the deciduous forests. Birds such as blue jays, woodpeckers, and thrushes fly

ARE YOU WEARING DEER PERFUME?

Male deer produce a liquid called *musk* inside a pouch behind their abdomens. Musk has a strong smell and is used to make perfumes. Hunting musk deer for this scented liquid has significantly decreased the deer's numbers.

Wolf

BROWN BEAR, BROWN BEAR, WHAT DO YOU SEE?

I see a Russian forest that's a perfect home for me. The brown bear is a symbol of Russia. This powerful animal weighs between 300 and 600 pounds. Its diet includes berries, fish, small animals, and honey.

Egrets

through the sky. Egrets, ducks, and other water birds swim in the marshes, lakes, and rivers in these forests. Snakes, lizards, and tortoises crawl along the forest floor and riverbanks.

The steppes are home to many small animals, including mice, rabbits, mole rats, and ground squirrels. Coyotes, antelope, badgers, weasels, and hawks prey on these small animals.

The steppe eagle makes its home in the grassy steppes. Because there are few trees on the steppes, these eagles nest on the ground. They are fierce hunters. Their prey includes mice, baby birds, lemmings, and other small animals.

The Caucasus and Ural Mountains are home to mountain goats, mountain sheep, wild boar, wild bison, and deer. Leopards and tigers can be spotted in these mountains as well.

Antelope

Mountain goat

SAVING RUSSIA'S ANIMALS

Russia has more than 150 nature preserves. The government runs these parks to save and protect endangered species.

15

CHAPTER 3

Looking Back Russia's History

SLAVIC STATES

The first people to settle in what is now Russia were Slavs. The Slavs hunted, fished, trapped, and farmed the land. They also set up trading centers. Different tribes of Slavs often fought with one another. Over time, these wars led to the formation of separate **states**. One group of Slavs was called the Varangians. About 1200 years ago, the Varangians established a state they called Rus. The capital of Rus was in Kiev, which is now a city in the Ukraine. Later, Rus became known as Russia.

Rus remained the most powerful state until 1240 when it was invaded by an Eastern tribe called the Tatars. The Tatars ruled Russia until 1480.

THE RISE OF THE TSARS

The city of Moscow was founded in 1147. Like the rest of Russia, Moscow was ruled by the Tatars between 1240 and 1480. In 1480, a Russian prince named Ivan III took control of Moscow and turned it into the most important city in western Russia. Ivan became known as Ivan the Great. His powerful armies defeated the Tatars and returned Russian rule to the Slavic people.

During this period, it was decided that the Russian prince in charge of the country would be known as the tsar. In 1547, Ivan the Great's son, Ivan IV, became the first tsar of Russia. Tsar Ivan IV united the different groups in Russia into one great nation. He built a powerful army and created a formal government to carry out his orders. The tsar also gave land to important people. These landholders remained loyal to Ivan throughout his rule.

In order to maintain wealth for the landowners and support the country's **economy**, Ivan IV established the system of **serfs**. Serfs worked for the landowners. They were charged very high taxes by the government and were not allowed to leave their masters or the land they worked on.

By the 1700s, Russia was one of the most powerful **empires** in the world. However, it was a land of great riches and great poverty. The tsars and landowners held all the wealth and power, while the serfs did all the work for little pay. These unfair conditions led to a great deal of anger. In time, this anger tore Russia apart.

> **FATHER OF RUSSIA**
> *Tsar* means "little father" in Russian. *Tsar* is sometimes spelled *czar* and is pronounced "zar."

> **IVAN THE TERRIBLE**
> Ivan IV was a smart ruler, but he was not a kind one. He had a terrible temper and killed many people, including his own son. Because of his cruelty, Ivan IV became known as "Ivan the Terrible."

THE RUSSIAN REVOLUTION

Between the 1700s and the early 1900s, several tsars tried to improve living conditions for serfs and other lower class Russians. Other tsars fought these attempts to **reform** the serf system. Several reformers were murdered or killed in battle. Others were **exiled** to Siberia.

In 1894, Nicholas II became tsar of Russia. Nicholas was a weak ruler who wasn't able to handle the increasing violence and demands for reform. His lack of control provided an opportunity for change.

A group of people called the Bolsheviks wanted to take power from the tsars and give it to the people. The Bolsheviks believed in communism. True communism is a system where all of a country's wealth and property is owned and shared by all of the people. The Bolsheviks were led by a man named Vladimir Lenin. Lenin wanted to get rid of the inequalities between the rich and poor people in Russia.

In 1914, Russia and many other countries fought in World War I. Russia suffered terribly during the war. Many people were killed. There was not enough food, fuel, or housing for everyone. Meanwhile, the tsar and other rich families continued to live well.

After hundreds of years of injustice, Russia's people had finally had enough.

Nicholas II

On March 8, 1917, factory workers, students, and other ordinary people protested. Fighting broke out between the crowds and the army. Finally, the government collapsed. Tsar Nicholas left the throne. He was arrested and later killed. The tsars no longer ruled Russia.

COMMUNISM AND THE USSR

After Tsar Nicholas left the throne, Russia was ruled by a temporary government. Then in November of 1917, the Bolsheviks led a **revolution** against the government. Several years of **civil war** followed. The Bolsheviks finally won control of the country. Vladimir Lenin became Russia's new leader.

A Bolshevik recruiting campaign

Vladimir Lenin

In 1922, the new government changed the name of the country to the Union of Soviet Socialist Republics (USSR). The Russian Republic was the largest of the republics under Bolshevik rule. Over the next few years, the USSR expanded to include many of the surrounding republics, such as the Ukraine, Tajikistan, Uzbekistan, Armenia, Georgia, and Kazakhstan.

Although communism was supposed to make everyone equal, it did not work that way. Instead, the government held all the power, while the people had none. Farmers were forced to turn over their crops to the government. Newspapers were controlled by the government. Any books, music, or art that the government did not approve of was not allowed. Anyone who spoke out against the Communists or their policies was exiled, jailed, or killed.

Lenin died in 1924. After several years of fighting over who would lead the country next, Joseph Stalin took control. Stalin ruled the USSR until his death in 1953. He was a brutal **dictator** who was feared by many. When people protested his new Communist policies, Stalin squashed them. He made up crimes against politicians who did not agree with him. He sent innocent people to labor camps, where they were held as prisoners. He ordered millions of people to be killed. The Russian people were so afraid of Stalin that they often turned in their friends and family to police to save themselves.

> **NAME CHANGES**
>
> The Union of Soviet Socialist Republics was also known as the USSR or the Soviet Union. The Russian people were called Soviets.
>
> During Communist rule, the country was also referred to as Soviet Russia. The time period was called the Soviet era or the Soviet period.

Joseph Stalin

In 1939, the USSR fought in World War II. After the war ended, the USSR took over many Eastern European countries. These countries were forced to have a Communist government and follow the USSR's orders. If a country tried to break free of Communist rule, the USSR sent its powerful army to crush the revolution.

1. Estonia
2. Latvia
3. Lithuania
4. Moldavia
5. Poland
6. Hungary
7. Bulgaria
8. Czechoslovakia
9. Romania
10. East Germany

The USSR and the United States had been friends during World War II. But after the war, the two nations became enemies. The United States did not support the USSR's government or the way it treated its people. Neither government trusted the other. Each country believed that the other might start another war to take control of the other. This period of fear and distrust was called the Cold War.

COMMUNIST EUROPE

During World War II, the USSR took control of Estonia, Latvia, Lithuania, and Moldavia. After the war, Poland, Hungary, Bulgaria, Czechoslovakia, Romania, and East Germany all fell under Communist control.

After Stalin's death, Russia had several Communist leaders. While conditions weren't as bad as during Stalin's rule, the government still held all the power. Soon poor management of this government led to many economic and political problems. Living conditions for many Russians continued to decline. Families waited years to get a small apartment. People had to wait in line to buy basic items of food like bread. By the late 1980s, the Soviet leaders realized it was time for a change.

Boris Yeltsin

THE FALL OF COMMUNISM

In 1985, Mikhail Gorbachev became the leader of the USSR. Gorbachev was open to new ideas. Slowly, he began to give the Russian people more freedom. He made many economic and social reforms.

During this time, people all over Eastern Europe were revolting against Communist governments. By the end of 1989, Communist governments in Poland, Hungary, Bulgaria, Romania, East Germany, and Czechoslovakia had fallen. People in Lithuania, Latvia, and Estonia fought to break free of the USSR and become independent.

Gorbachev tried to stop the breakup of the USSR, but it was too late. In 1991, other members of the government tried to overthrow Gorbachev. Eventually he resigned as the leader of the Communist Party, and Boris Yeltsin took control of the government. Yeltsin ended Communist rule and appointed himself president of Russia. The Union of Soviet Socialist Republics was divided into 15 separate republics. Russia was once again an independent nation.

MODERN RUSSIA

In 1993, Russian voters approved a new **constitution**. The Russian Federation is now a democratic government with three branches. The executive branch is headed by an elected president. The legislature has two houses—the Federation Council and the State Duma. The judicial branch is the country's court system.

Although the Russian people have much more freedom than they did under Communist rule, the difficulties are far from over. The change from communism to democracy continues to challenge the country today. However, democratic rule has eased much of the tension between Russia and other nations of the world.

ON THEIR OWN

At the time of its breakup, the USSR's 15 republics were Russia, Ukraine, Belarus, Armenia, Azerbaijan, Kazakhstan, Kyrgyzstan, Moldova, Tajikistan, Turkmenistan, Uzbekistan, Georgia, Latvia, Lithuania, and Estonia. All of these republics are now independent countries.

CHAPTER 4
Digging In to Russia's Resources and Industries

Russia has an abundance of natural resources. Almost every major mineral found on Earth is produced in the country. Manufacturing and other industrial efforts are the main focus of the economy. Forestry, agriculture, and fishing are also important sources of income.

MINERALS

Russia has enormous mineral **deposits**. The country is one of the world's largest producers of nickel. Iron and aluminum **ore** are found in the northern part of the country. Copper, iron, tin, gold, lead, and precious gemstones lie beneath the Ural Mountains.

Iron

WHICH WAY DO I GO?

There is so much iron near Kursk in European Russia that it makes compasses read incorrectly. Compasses use the magnetic field of the Earth to determine directions. Iron is a magnetic metal. Large amounts of this metal under the ground interfere with the Earth's magnetic field, causing compasses to swerve off course.

ENERGY

Russia has tremendous amounts of coal, oil, and natural gas deposits. However, the majority of these fuels are located under the frozen land of Siberia. The harsh climate and conditions there make it expensive to remove these resources from the ground. Special machinery that can withstand the cold must be used. Employees are paid higher wages to work in these tough conditions.

Most of Russia's energy is supplied by the burning of coal, oil, and gas. The country also has **nuclear** power plants. These plants provide about 15 percent of the country's electricity needs. Hydroelectric plants along major rivers such as the Volga also provide power to Russian homes and businesses.

> **THE BIG MELTDOWN**
>
> Workers in Siberia often use high-pressure steam hoses to melt the frozen land so they can reach the gas and oil deposits underneath.

FORESTRY AND AGRICULTURE

Russia has the largest area of coniferous forests in the world. Its taigas provide timber for building and constructing wood products. The trees are also used to make paper.

Russia has immense areas of fertile land. The country's main crops are barley, wheat, corn, oats, rye, sugar beets, potatoes, and tea. Sheep, pigs, and cattle are raised in European Russia. In northern Siberia, some people raise reindeer for meat and fur.

During the Soviet era, the government controlled farm production. The government paid so little for crops that farmers had little reason to grow a lot of crops or use modern equipment. As a result, Russia's farms are still not as productive as they could be.

Wheat

FISHING

Fishing is an important part of Russia's economy. The country has large fleets of fishing ships in the Baltic and White Seas, as well as the Atlantic and Pacific Oceans. Many of Russia's rivers and lakes are a source of seafood as well. Cod, herring, salmon, carp, chub, and sturgeon are a few of the common catches in Russia.

MANUFACTURING, SERVICES, AND TRADE

Many Russian cities are surrounded by factories and industrial centers. The country is home to some of the world's largest steel mills. There are also many automobile and truck factories. St. Petersburg is a major center for shipbuilding. Other cities produce electrical equipment, construction materials, and machinery.

Despite the large number of manufacturing industries, many of these factories are poorly run and have out-of-date equipment. This makes it hard for Russia to compete with other nations that have more modern equipment and methods.

Many Russians work in service industries, such as banking, restaurants, hotels, and stores. Since the fall of communism, Russians have been encouraged to own and run their own businesses. In addition, the government wants to return all government-run farms and businesses to private owners. These changes have been difficult for workers and for the country's economy. However, Russian stores now have a greater variety and number of goods than they did during the Soviet era.

Russia does most of its trading with Germany and other European countries. The United States, China, and Japan are also important trading partners. Russia **imports** much of its machinery, medicines, **consumer goods**, and food. It **exports** minerals, oil, natural gas, timber, and metals.

FISH EGGS, ANYONE?
Sturgeon are large fish that produce many eggs. These eggs can be made into an expensive treat called *caviar*. Caviar is a soft, salty spread that is often eaten on crackers.

TIME TO SHOP
Moscow now has more than 250 supermarkets.

CHAPTER 5

The Many Faces of Russia

Discovering Russia's People

Almost 145 million people live in Russia. Most of them live in European Russia, where the land and climate are less harsh and resources are more readily available.

Russia is a blend of many different **cultures** and **ethnic** groups. About 80 percent of the people are ethnic Russians. The other 20 percent belong to more than 100 different ethnic groups, such as Tatars, Ukrainians, and Moldovans.

The largest split in the population is still the division between the rich and the poor. While opportunities have widened for workers, there are still huge inequalities between the upper and lower classes in the country.

LIFE IN THE CITIES

Since the end of World War II, many people have moved from the countryside into the cities in search of better jobs and a higher standard of living. About 75 percent of Russia's people now live in **urban** areas.

Russian cities are very crowded. Most families live in small apartments located in high-rise buildings. A typical Russian apartment has two bedrooms, a small living and dining room, one bathroom, and a kitchen. Because apartments are hard to find, many family members, including grandparents, parents, children, and other

St. Petersburg

relatives, often live together. Sometimes two families share one apartment.

Rich city dwellers normally live in apartments too, but they often have a house in the country as well. These houses are called *dachas*. Dachas provide a place for families to go on weekends and for vacations during the summer. City residents also use the land around their dachas to grow vegetable gardens.

BIG CITY FACTS

- Moscow is Russia's largest city. Nearly nine million people make their home there. Moscow became the capital of the country in 1918 and continues to be the site of the government today.
- St. Petersburg is Russia's second largest city and the country's largest seaport. St. Petersburg has had several names. It was originally named St. Petersburg when it was founded by Peter the Great in 1703. After World War I, the name was changed to Petrograd. After the death of Vladimir Lenin, it became Leningrad. In 1991, it finally returned to its original name.

Dacha

Russian city streets are very busy. People crowd into stores or buy food, clothes, and supplies from booths set up on the sidewalk. Food and other supplies are very expensive in Russia. Product shortages often exist.

Few people in Russia can afford a car. Instead, they get around using buses, trains, and subways.

Arbat Street pedestrian mall in Moscow

UNDERGROUND ART
Moscow's subway stations are very beautiful. The stations have tiled walls, paintings, and even chandeliers!

LIFE IN THE COUNTRY

About 25 percent of Russia's people live in **rural** areas. Many live in small wooden houses in large villages. People travel from these villages to work on nearby farms. Many country houses have no electricity or running water. The roads are not paved and become muddy or snowy whenever a storm passes through.

Rural Russians have few modern conveniences. Hospitals and doctors are scarce. Schools are poor and lack supplies. Libraries, computers, and other resources aren't available in most areas. Rural Russian families must also grow their own food and provide their own milk, meat, and eggs.

CHAPTER 6

A Slice of Life
Russian Culture

Russia's political and economic history have greatly affected the culture of the country. Most old Russian traditions were not honored during the Communist era as leaders tried to form their own culture. In recent years, reviving traditions and celebrations has become important to restoring hope to millions of citizens. The mix of ethnic groups and cultures has contributed unique flavor to Russian life as well.

FOOD

The Russian diet mainly consists of a few basic foods. Bread and cereals are found at almost all Russian meals. Kasha, a cooked breakfast cereal made of buckwheat, is eaten at breakfast tables across the country. Russians also eat a lot of potatoes, cabbage, and fish.

Russia is known for several special foods. Blinis are thin pancakes filled with jelly or sour cream or wrapped around small pieces of fish or other meat. Pirozhkis are meat or vegetable dumplings that are baked or fried. Borscht originally came from the Ukraine. This soup is made of beets, cabbage, and meat, with a scoop of sour cream on top.

Most Russians drink milk or tea. Adults drink a kind of beer called *kvass*, which is made from bread and honey. An alcoholic drink called *vodka* is the national drink enjoyed by many adults.

Blinis

Over the past ten years, American food has moved into Russia. It isn't hard to find fast-food restaurants such as McDonald's or Pizza Hut in Russia's major cities. Most Russians, however, cannot afford to eat out in expensive restaurants. Instead, cheaper cafes are popular places. These small restaurants serve food and drinks. In the evening, they are often crowded with Russians watching TV and meeting with their friends.

TEATIME IN RUSSIA

The Chinese introduced tea to Russia in the early 17th century. Since then, tea has remained a common drink in the country. Special teapots called *samovars* can be found in many Russian homes. Below are two recipes for your own Russian tea party.

RUSSIAN TEA CAKES

ingredients

1 cup butter
1 teaspoon vanilla
6 tablespoons + 1 cup powdered sugar
2 cups flour
1 cup chopped walnuts

directions

1. Preheat oven to 350°.
2. Cream butter and vanilla until smooth. Combine the 6 tablespoons of sugar and the flour. Stir into the butter mixture. Add the walnuts and mix until blended.
3. Roll the dough into 1-inch balls. Place them 2 inches apart on an ungreased cookie sheet.
4. Bake cookies for 10–12 minutes until set but not brown.
5. Roll the warm cookies in the cup of powdered sugar. When cool, roll the balls in the sugar again.

RUSSIAN TEA

ingredients

1¼ cup dry orange-flavored instant breakfast drink (like Tang)
½ cup sugar
⅓ cup instant tea
½ teaspoon ground cinnamon
¼ teaspoon ground cloves
dash of salt

directions

1. Mix all of the ingredients together.
2. Place 2½ teaspoons of the mixture in a cup, and add 8 ounces of boiling water. Drink hot or add ice cubes to chill.

CLOTHING

During the Soviet era, Russian clothes were plain and poorly made. Buyers had no choice of style or color. Today, most Russians wear the same clothes as people in Europe and North America. Because most of Russia has such a cold climate, sweaters, heavy coats, hats, gloves, and scarves are important items of clothing. Some ethnic groups have kept their traditional styles of dress. Men wear white shirts with fancy embroidered designs on the front, while women wear colorful dresses or skirts and headdresses. Older women often cover their heads with scarves called *babushkas*.

GRANDMA'S SCARF

Babushka is also the Russian word for "grandmother." The scarves known as babushkas got their name because they are often worn by grandmothers and other older women.

EDUCATION

Russian children must attend school from ages 7 to 16. Children in grades one through four attend primary schools. Children in grades five through nine attend middle schools. Students at the first two levels take science, math, reading, writing, social studies, and physical fitness.

When students finish middle school, they take a national test. Students who do well attend high schools called *secondary schools*. Secondary school students focus on one subject, such as math or literature. Students who do not do as well on the exam can go to vocational school. Here the students learn a trade, such as how to fix cars.

HIGH GOALS FOR READING AND WRITING

The Communist government placed a high emphasis on education. It wanted skilled workers who believed in Communist ideals. Because of this, the country has a 99 percent literacy rate today. This means that almost all of the adult population in Russia can read and write.

Only about 25 percent of Russian students continue their education past secondary school. Secondary school graduates must pass a difficult test to gain admission to a university or medical school. These schools have five-year programs that train students for a specific profession.

Education is taken very seriously in Russia. Most students attend school six days a week. The school day begins at 8:00 in the morning and ends at 2:00 in the afternoon. The teachers are strict and assign a lot of homework. In poor areas, where there isn't enough space or supplies, students attend school in shifts.

During the Soviet era, the government controlled all textbooks. Students learned only what the government wanted them to learn. Often the government hid unpleasant facts or information that made the country look bad. Students were expected to memorize what their teachers told them and could not ask questions or give opinions.

After the fall of communism, there was more freedom in Russian education. Now students are encouraged to ask questions. Instead of reciting facts, teachers lead students in discussions and hands-on activities. Most schools now have new books that tell the real story of Russian history.

> **TOTAL CONTROL**
>
> The Communist government didn't just control school books. It also controlled television, radio, and newspapers. Russian TV didn't even have commercials until the late 1980s.

SPORTS AND LEISURE ACTIVITIES

Soccer is the most popular sport in Russia. Most large towns and cities have soccer stadiums or fields, and many adults and children play this fast-paced game. Volleyball, basketball, weight lifting, skiing, and swimming are also enjoyed by many Russians.

Russia's cold climate is perfect for hockey. The Russian hockey team is one of the best in the world. Several Russians have played for American and Canadian teams in the National Hockey League. These players include Pavel Bure, Slava Fetisov, and Alexander Mogilny.

Russian athletes have always done well at the Olympic Games. During Soviet rule, top athletes were supported by the government so they could spend their lives training to be the best. Ekaterina Gordeyeva, Oksana Baiul, and Victor Petrenko are among the many Russian figure skaters who have become famous around the world. Gymnasts such as Olga Korbut have also risen to the top of their sport. Since Russia became a free country, the government hasn't been able to support athletes as much as it had in the past. Still, many Russian athletes have succeeded at the Olympics and other international sporting events.

Olympic Stadium in Russia

A COUNTRY WITHOUT A FLAG

During the 1992 Summer and Winter Olympics, athletes from Russia and the other 14 countries that had once made up the Soviet Union competed as the Unified Team. Since the Unified Team had no national flag, its athletes carried the Olympic flag instead. And since they had no national anthem, a piece of classical music was played whenever a Unified Team athlete won a medal.

Chess is a board game played by Russians. Many chess champions like Gary Kasparov and Anatoly Karpov have come from the country. Russian children learn to play chess in school. It is common to see Russians playing chess in public parks.

Going to the circus is a fun-filled event for many Russians. Almost every city has a circus. Tickets are cheap enough so that everyone can attend performances.

> **UNDER THE BIG TOP**
> With more than 7000 performers, the Moscow Circus is the largest circus in Russia. This circus has toured all over the world.

RELIGION

For centuries, many Russians belonged to the Russian Orthodox Church. However, during most of the Soviet era, practicing religion was against the law and most churches closed. In the late 1980s, the government relaxed the laws against religion. The Russian people were free to worship as they pleased. Today, there are more than 5000 Russian Orthodox churches in Russia.

Other religions are practiced in Russia as well. More than 500,000 Jews live in the country. Other citizens are Lutheran, Baptist, or Roman Catholic. Moscow and parts of southern Russia have large populations of Muslims.

Church of the Resurrection of Christ in St. Petersburg

> **RELIGIOUS ATTACKS**
> During the late 1800s and early 1900s, the tsar's army attacked Jewish villages and murdered many Jews. These attacks were called *pogroms*. Millions of Jews left Russia and **emigrated** to the United States to escape the pogroms.

35

HOLIDAYS

Russians celebrate a variety of religious and national holidays. During Communist rule, religious holidays were outlawed. After 1991, traditional religious celebrations sprung up again. Russians celebrate Christmas (January 7) and Easter (March or April). These celebrations are marked by family gatherings, church services, and special foods.

New Year's Day (January 1) is the most popular holiday in Russia. Families and friends get together to share a meal and celebrate the new year. When Christmas was banned, many citizens added Christmas traditions, such as giving presents, decorating trees, and getting gifts from Father Frost, to their New Year's celebrations. Now these events have become part of both Christmas and New Year's festivities.

May 1 is Spring and Labour Day. Under Communist rule, this day was a time for the government to show off its tanks and military equipment in huge parades. Today, Spring and Labour Day is a time for families to enjoy parades and visit friends.

The decoration and exchange of eggs is an important Easter tradition in Russia.

Several of Russia's holidays honor important political events in the country's history. February 23 is Soldier's Day, a day to remember Russia's soldiers. International Women's Day on March 8 is a tribute to the women's rights movement of the early 1900s. May 9 is Victory Day, which marks the end of World War I. Constitution Day takes place on December 12, the day that the new constitution of the Russian Federation was approved in 1993. Russia's newest holiday is June 12—Independence Day. This day celebrates the beginning of the Russian Federation and the end of Communist rule.

ARTS

The arts have always been woven into Russian life. The country is known for its great writers, musicians, dancers, and artists.

The years between 1820 and 1890 are called the Golden Age of Russian literature. Alexander Pushkin, who lived from 1799 until 1837, is considered the founder of modern Russian literature. Pushkin wrote many poems and fairy tales. He is still one of Russia's most beloved writers.

Fyodor Dostoyevsky and Leo Tolstoy also lived during Russia's Golden Age. Dostoyevsky wrote *Crime and Punishment* and other books about crimes and their effects on people. Tolstoy wrote about war and love. His most famous novel was *War and Peace*. These books have influenced people all over the world.

During the years of Soviet rule, writers were forced to write positive things about the government and daily life in Russia. Anyone who refused could be sent to prison or forced to leave the country. In 1958, Russian novelist Boris Pasternak won the Nobel Prize in literature for his novel *Doctor Zhivago*.

Leo Tolstoy

This novel was set during the Russian Revolution. Because the government thought *Doctor Zhivago* was anti-Soviet, they refused to let Pasternak accept the prize. The book was not published in Russia until years after Pasternak died.

Alexander Solzhenitsyn was another writer who suffered for speaking out against the government. His novel, *The Life and Times of Ivan Denisovich*, won the Nobel Prize for literature in 1970. This book was based on Solzhenitsyn's time in a Soviet labor camp. After the publication of his book, Solzhenitsyn was forced to leave Russia. Twenty years later, he was finally able to return home.

The 1800s were also a golden age for Russian music. During this time, composers such as Peter Ilych Tchaikovsky, Modest Mussorgsky, and Nikolay Rimsky-Korsakov thrilled Russian audiences. Their music included melodies from Russian folk songs and told stories based on Russia's history and legends.

Like writers, musicians were told to write cheerful music during the Soviet period. Despite government pressure, composers such as Igor Stravinsky, Sergey Prokofiev, and Sergey Rachmaninoff wrote complex music that showed the sadness and anger that many Russians felt. Today, Russians enjoy many different types of music, including folk music, opera, and rock and roll.

Igor Stravinsky

Russian music features many native instruments. A *balalaika* is similar to a guitar. It is shaped like a triangle and has only three strings. The *gusli* is a harp that has been played since ancient times.

Many classical Russian composers wrote music for the ballet. Russia is home to some

NO INSTRUMENTS ALLOWED

Before the 1600s, the Russian Orthodox Church did not allow any music except for the human singing voice.

> **DANCING TO A NEW LAND**
>
> During the Soviet era, several ballet dancers **defected** from Russia to live in countries with more freedom. Rudolf Nureyev, Mikhail Baryshnikov, and Natalia Makarova are three dancers who left their homeland to live and work in America and Europe.

Mikhail Baryshnikov

the finest ballet companies in the world. The Kirov Ballet in Petersburg and the Bolshoi Ballet Moscow are known all over the world for their fine dancers and beautiful performances. Ballet is still very popular Russia. Dancers are admired like movie stars are in the United States.

Russian art has awed viewers for thousands of years. Religious paintings called *icons* are a unique form of Russian art. Icons are religious images painted on small wooden panels.

Born in Moscow, Wassily Kandinsky combined his love of music and painting into **abstract art**. His colorful visions led him to become known as the founder of modern abstract painting.

During the 1900s, Russian-born painter Marc Chagall became recognized around the world for his expressive, brightly colored paintings. Chagall's paintings often included images from Russian folktales.

> **RUSSIAN PEASANT ART**
>
> Have you ever seen a set of wooden dolls that fit inside one another? These dolls are called *matryosh* or *nesting dolls*. The original dolls were decorated like Russian peasants, but today, a wide variety of people important to Russian culture are painted on these dolls.

CHAPTER 7

What's Ahead?
A Look at Russia's Future

Russia has faced centuries of war, violence, oppressive governments, and economic struggles. Today, its people have more freedom and opportunities, but the future still holds many challenges.

ECONOMIC TROUBLES

During the Communist era, the government kept prices low and provided jobs for almost every citizen. Workers were guaranteed a job for life. After the fall of communism, Russia began moving toward a **capitalist** economy. Suddenly, prices were based on supply and demand, and jobs were based on production levels. Outdated factories could not compete with goods made in other countries that used modern machinery. Many businesses closed, and many Russians lost their jobs.

Russia's leaders now want to return all farms and businesses to private owners. Although this type of economy will most likely be better in the long run, it has been difficult to change the practices of the past 80 years. Although the Russian people have responded eagerly to the challenges and freedoms of owning their own businesses, it will be many years before the economy is stable. In the meantime, poverty, unemployment, homelessness, and hunger continue to trouble the nation.

> **SLOW RIDE**
> In the mid-1990s, a Japanese factory could build a car 30 times faster than a Russian factory could.

FIGHTING FOR FREEDOM

The end of communism did not mean the end of political problems. Russia has continued to struggle as ethnic groups demand a voice in the country's government. Some ethnic groups have demanded complete independence from Russia. In 1994, Russia sent troops to a region called Chechnya because Chechnyans were revolting from Russian rule. In spite of peace agreements, violence and terrorist attacks have continued.

THE ENVIRONMENT

The Russian environment suffered terribly under Communist rule. Inefficient factories dumped poisonous chemicals that seeped into the air, water, and land. Habitat destruction resulted in the decrease or loss of plant and animal species.

Nuclear power plants and nuclear waste from ships have also damaged the environment. In 1986, an accident at the Chernobyl nuclear plant in the Ukraine released **radiation** into the area. Many plants and animals were killed, especially coniferous trees and small mammals. While the environment is on its way to recovery, the incident at Chernobyl was a deadly warning about the effects of energy sources on the environment.

MORE DEADLY EFFECTS

The accident at Chernobyl affected more than just the environment. Thirty-one people were killed immediately by the accident. Thousands more have died of cancer and other illnesses related to radiation poisoning.

Thousands of wooden crosses stand next to the Chernobyl plant to honor the victims of the nuclear disaster.

41

In recent years, Russia has begun to repair the damages. Many groups have established programs to clean up the environment, find safer forms of energy, and protect endangered plant and animal life. However, years of damage to this huge country will take time to heal.

LOOKING FORWARD

No one is sure what Russia's future holds. Some people believe the country can return to its position as a world power, with its people thriving under a democratic government and a capitalist economy. Others worry that the nation will be unable to meet the huge demands of its large population and the enormous changes that have occurred since 1991.

Despite the uncertainty of tomorrow, Russia will continue to move forward. Its rich culture, dramatic history, and determined people will help Russia mend the nation and the hearts of its people.

SAVING A LAKE

During the 1950s, a paper mill poured toxic chemicals into Lake Baikal. Chemicals from nearby farms also flowed into the water. By the 1980s, the lake was so polluted that many of its animals and plants were dying. Since the 1990s, Russia's government has been taking steps to save the lake, but it will take time to restore the lake's health.

The Kremlin and St. Basil's Church are spotlighted in Moscow's darkness. The Kremlin is the center of Russian government.